PETS AND MORE PETS

Compiled by the CHILD STUDY ASSOCIATION OF AMERICA:

Read-to-Me Storybook
Read Me Another Story
Read Me More Stories
Holiday Storybook
Read-to-Yourself Storybook
More Read-to-Yourself Stories:
  Fun and Magic
Castles and Dragons:
  Read-to-Yourself Fairy Tales
  for Boys and Girls
Read to Me Again
Now You Can Read to Yourself
Round About the City:
  Stories You Can Read to Yourself
Pets and More Pets:
  Read-to-Yourself Stories of the City

12

Read-to-Yourself
Stories of the City

PETS AND MORE PETS

Selected by
the Child Study
Association of
America

Illustrated by
Michael Hampshire

Thomas Y. Crowell Company *New York*

Grateful acknowledgment is made to the following for permission to reprint copyrighted matter in this book:

Ellen F. Bloom: "New Pets for Kate" by Ellen F. Bloom, copyright © 1969 by Child Study Association of America.

Nelle Graham Brooks: "Who Wants Gerbils?" by Nelle Graham Brooks, copyright © 1969 by Child Study Association of America.

Doubleday & Company, Inc.: "The Best Birthday" by Quail Hawkins, copyright © 1954 by Quail Hawkins.

Follett Publishing Company: "Henry" by Elizabeth Vreeken, copyright © 1961 by Follett Publishing Co.; "The Dog Who Came to Dinner" by Sydney Taylor, copyright © 1966 by Follett Publishing Co.

Golden Press, Inc.: "Where's Willie?" by Seymour Reit, copyright © 1960 by Golden Press, Inc.

Harcourt, Brace & World, Inc.: "Twenty-four Cakes of Flea Soap" from *Betsey and the Boys* by Carolyn Haywood, copyright 1945 by Harcourt, Brace & World, Inc.

Alfred A. Knopf, Inc.: "Muggsy" by Marion Holland, copyright © 1959 by Marion Holland and Theresa Sherman.

William Morrow and Company, Inc.: "Gallons of Guppies" from *Henry Huggins* by Beverly Cleary, copyright © 1959 by William Morrow and Company, Inc.

Western Publishing Company, Inc., Racine, Wisc.: "Peppermint" by Dorothy Grider, copyright © 1950 by Western Publishing Company, Inc.

 Manufactured in the United States of America. L.C. Card 69-11825. ISBN 0-690-61661-9; 0-690-61662-7 (LB). Published in Canada by Fitzhenry & Whiteside Limited, Toronto.

3 4 5 6 7 8 9 10

This book is affectionately dedicated to

Sidonie Matsner Gruenberg,

whose love of children and children's books started the work of the Children's Book Committee fifty years ago.

CONTENTS

PETS AND MORE PETS

Who Wants Gerbils?

by Nelle Graham Brooks

Randy came home from school with Max.

The gerbils heard the boys coming. They had been sleeping in their juice can on the lower floor of their cage-house in Max's room. Now the pair, looking like tiny squirrels, sat up, wet their front paws with their tongues, and hurriedly washed their faces. Then they scrambled through the cedar chips on the floor of their cage, jumped on top of the juice can, and climbed

through the hole above into the upper room of their cage-house.

When the boys came in, the gerbils were sitting like tiny kangaroos, as close as they could get to the cage door, peering this way and that, trying to see if the boys were bringing their afternoon snack. They hopped up and down impatiently while the boys got sunflower seeds from a can on the window sill.

Randy often came home with Max to help him feed his gerbils. (Max told him gerbils sounds like jurbils.) Each boy held a seed by the smallest end and handed it through the wires of the cage to the gerbil. Each gerbil took a seed carefully from the boy's fingers with its teeth. They cracked off the shells; then they ate the kernel, holding it in their front paws as a squirrel eats a nut.

Randy never got tired of watching Max's gerbils. He loved watching them eat corn flakes one at a time, nibbling off the edge, round and round. He had often wished that he had gerbils of his own. And now he could hardly believe he was going to have them—not just any old gerbils, but *these* gerbils, Jerry and Jenny.

The boys tried three different shopping bags before they found one big enough to put the two-story house into. It was the biggest shopping bag they had ever seen, a special Christmas shopping bag, bright red and green. They lifted the cage into it carefully as Max said good-bye to Jerry and Jenny. At last Randy started home, carefully holding the huge shopping bag.

As Randy pushed open the front door of his house his mother said, "Where did you ever get that huge shopping bag? What's in it?"

Three smaller children came dancing to the door.

"Let us see, Randy. What do you have?"

"Wait," said Randy, "Just wait until I get it out and you will see."

Randy lifted the gerbil cage out of the bag and put it on the table.

"Rats!" gasped his mother. "Get those rats right out of my house."

"But they're *not* rats," said Randy, "they're gerbils, a kind of jumping desert mouse."

"Gerbils, mice, or rats," said his mother, "get them right out of this house. Wherever did you get them?"

"Max gave them to me for a going-away present. I thought if you saw how cute they are, you would let me keep them."

"With three small children in the house? No, Randy, I'm afraid you'll have to take them right back to Max."

"Please, mom," pleaded Randy. "Just these two!"

"There's only *one* gerbil," said five-year-old Caroline. She was peering into the cage.

"I knew it," said mother. "Who opened that cage door? You let one get out!"

"I didn't," said three voices at once.

"Then how did it get out?" asked mother. "Shut the door to the hall quickly. Shut both doors. I'll get the broom."

Mother was back in three seconds.

"Look under the table. Each of you look under a chair," she ordered as she swished the broom under the sofa.

"What do we do if we see it?" asked seven-year-old Chris. "Do we just pick it up?"

"I won't pick it up!" said mother. "Randy, how do we catch it?"

"I see it," squealed Caroline. But Caroline was not looking under a chair. She was still looking into the cage. And sure enough, there was Jenny, coming up from under a pile of cedar chips where she had been rooting around, looking for seeds which she had buried for safekeeping. She shook the cedar chips off the top of her head and wiped a few off her whiskers.

"Isn't she cute?" said Randy. "Please may I keep them?"

"I have to admit she's cute," said mother. "I'm sorry, Randy, but she can't stay here. She wasn't out this time, but she could be. Someone would be sure to open the cage door."

"I wouldn't." "I wouldn't." "I

wouldn't," promised three children. "Please let the gerbils stay."

"I'm very sorry, but no. They must go back to Max right this minute."

So Randy sadly put the cage back into the big shopping bag and went back to Max's house. It was Max's mother who let him in.

"My mother wouldn't let me keep Jerry and Jenny," he explained.

"You mean you didn't ask your mother before you took them, Randy? Oh, dear, now what do we do?"

"If Randy can't keep my gerbils," pleaded Max, "can't I keep them myself? Can't I take them with me?"

"It's too bad," said mother, "but you just can't. We are stopping many places on our way to Uganda. And we have no idea what kind of place we'll live in when we get there. You will have to find someone else to take Jerry and Jenny."

Next day Max went to school a little early. The first boy he saw was Chubby. "Chubby, would you like to have my gerbils?" Max asked.

"No pets for me," said Chubby.

"But gerbils aren't much trouble," argued Max. "You don't have to walk them like a dog. You don't have to remember to put them out at night like cats."

"That's not it," explained Chubby. "You have to buy things for pets, like food. We have a rule in our family that whoever has a pet, has to buy what the pet needs out of his own allowance."

"But gerbils need hardly anything," argued Max. "Gerbils eat mostly seeds.

I dry all the seeds from our kitchen—melon seeds, squash seeds, apple seeds. But not orange seeds—they're too bitter. I only buy sunflower seeds."

"That's just it," said Chubby. "Sunflower seeds. I'd rather spend my allowance on candy."

Tim was coming across the school yard. "Hi, Tim," called Max, and ran to meet him. "Would you like to have my gerbils?"

"They're a kind of mouse, aren't they?" asked Tim. "They wouldn't last a day at my house. We have a cat—she's trained to catch mice. Gerbils or mice, they'd be all the same to our cat."

"Thanks for telling me," said Max. "I wouldn't give Jerry and Jenny to you if you paid me."

Just then Vicky came along. Max thought Vicky was the nicest girl in his class. "Would you like my gerbils, Vicky?" he asked. Then he wished he hadn't. Too late he remembered that girls hate mice.

"Pee-uuu," said Vicky. "Stinky animals, no thank you."

"But Jerry and Jenny are not *stinky animals,*" insisted Max. "They don't smell any worse than birds."

Vicky just held her nose, said

"Pee-uuu, Pee-uuu," and walked away.

It was time to go into the classroom. Max went along with the other children. Jerry and Jenny were still on his mind. He just had to find a home for them today. As soon as he got into the classroom he said in a loud voice, "Wouldn't anyone in this *whole* room like two gerbils for pets?"

"I would," said a small voice over in the corner. "I would like pets. Are they small, for a small apartment?"

All the children looked over at Sugu, the new boy in class. He had come from Japan only the week before. He was timid about trying to speak in English. He was timid about trying to play games that were strange to him. None of the children knew him very well yet. He was the very last person Max would ever have thought of asking to take the gerbils. He must really want the gerbils, to be brave enough to speak out in the whole class.

Max hurried over to Sugu. "Gerbils are small," he said, "hardly bigger than mice. And they eat mostly seeds, which don't cost much. They are not smelly. They are not noisy. They make only tiny squeaks."

Max talked fast, trying to tell Sugu why gerbils were the perfect pet, before Sugu would change his mind about wanting Jerry and Jenny. But Sugu didn't need to be sold the idea. Sugu wanted a pet, any pet, very much. He had not been allowed to bring his pet dog from Japan with him. He was lonesome in this strange place.

"I will like the gerbils," he said. "When I go home to lunch I will ask my mother if I can take them."

When school was out in the afternoon Sugu's mother came to meet him. Sugu and his mother walked home with Max. Max's mother and Sugu's mother talked together in the living room. Sugu and Max spent a long time in Max's room. Max told Sugu how to feed his pets.

He showed him how to move the gerbils from the cage to a large carton, where they could play while the cage was being cleaned. He showed Sugu how to take the cage apart and clean it.

Then the gerbils, in their clean house, were gently put into the huge shopping bag once more. Max scribbled something on a paper. He handed the paper to Sugu. "Here's my new address in Uganda," he said. "You must write and tell me how Jerry and Jenny are."

"I will," said Sugu, "and you must write to me. Maybe you will get a new pet to write to me about."

"Mother," called Max, "Sugu and I and the gerbils are going to be pen pals."

New Pets for Kate

by Ellen F. Bloom

Kate was always in a hurry. When she wanted to do something she wanted to do it that minute. She couldn't wait. She talked fast because she had so many things to say.

"Do try to talk more slowly, dear," her grandmother would say. "You swallow your words."

This made Kate laugh. How could you swallow things like *words?*

When she rushed across the room to get something she usually knocked things over.

She dressed in a hurry and never quite closed the bureau drawers. She tied her shoes in a hurry, so they always came untied during the day. She dropped her clothes on the floor because there was always something more interesting to do than to pick them up.

On school days she ran down to Davy's apartment, just below hers. They were both in the second grade, and they walked to school together.

The only time Kate didn't hurry was with her little brother Ken. He was four years old and he needed time to think about things. Kate loved him very much.

One Saturday afternoon the doorbell rang. When her mother opened the door Kate heard a beloved voice. "Aunt Betsy!" she shrieked. She ran to the hall and flung her arms around her aunt. A

white cardboard box flew out of her aunt's hands to the floor.

"Goodness, Kate," said Aunt Betsy clapping her hand to her forehead. "I hope they are still alive."

Kate pounced on the little box.

"What in the world can be alive in this? It looks like an ice-cream box."

She opened the top and looked inside. Two tiny turtles were there. One was light green, the other a little darker. With a squeal of joy Kate gave Aunt Betsy a big hug.

"I never had a pet before," she said. "What do they eat?"

Aunt Betsy opened another package and took out a plastic bowl with a place for water and a tiny plastic tree on a little island. She gave Kate a box of turtle food.

"Let's put them in the bowl," said Aunt Betsy. Kate got a glass of water. She dripped some on the rug as she hurried back to put it in the bowl.

Ken was looking at the turtles with their tiny feet and tiny heads and beady eyes. He put out his chubby finger very slowly to touch one.

Quick as a wink the head and feet

and even the tail disappeared into the round shell. Ken's big blue eyes opened wide with surprise.

"That's the way turtles do," said Kate, kneeling beside Ken. "The little shell is their house. They feel safe in there. Watch them poke their heads and feet out again." And, sure enough, as they waited, that is exactly what happened.

Kate picked up the larger one very gently.

"Look at his eyes, Kenny," said Aunt Betsy. "They are tinier than the top of a pin. And look at the red spots where his ears are, and the little collar that covers his head when he pulls it in."

Ken laughed with delight as he picked up the little one and turned it over. He pointed to the yellow underside of the shell and counted with his fingers five little circles.

Mother came in with a plate of cookies. Kate spun around so fast that the turtle fell out of her hand. He lay on his back with his tiny feet waving in the air and couldn't move. Tears came to Kate's eyes as she knelt down and gently picked him up. "Poor turtle, I hope you aren't hurt." But when she put him back in the bowl and he moved around so fast, she knew he was all right.

When Aunt Betsy left, Kate hurried down to Davy's apartment. She rushed toward his room calling, "Guess what I have? Guess what I just got?"

Davy was sitting up in his bed. He had a cold, so Kate talked to him from the hall.

"What is it, what have you got?"

"Guess," said Kate. "You can have five questions and three guesses."

"Is it something to eat?" asked Davy, who was usually hungry.

"No."

"Is it something to wear?"

"No."

"Is it something to sit on?"

Kate giggled. "No," she said again. "They move."

"They?" asked Davy. "It must be—is it alive?"

"YES," said Kate. "It is two things

alive and they are in a bo—" Then she put her hand over her mouth so she wouldn't finish the word.

"Does it—I mean do they make noise?"

"That is your last question and they are ab-so-lute-ly quiet. Now guess."

"Well they can't be puppies or kittens. Are they hamsters?"

"NO—two more guesses."

"Are they goldfish?"

"Wrong."

"Are they earthworms?" Davy shouted and fell on his back on the bed laughing because he knew that Kate ab-so-lute-ly hated them.

"No. They are turtles. One is light green and one is dark, and they have tiny eyes and they eat ant eggs, and Aunt Betsy just brought them to me and you have to see them when your cold is finished." And Kate left as fast as she had come.

By Monday Davy's cold was better. He promised to come and see the turtles after school.

In school Kate told all about her turtles and her teacher asked if the children knew that fable about the race between the hare and the tortoise. She explained that a hare was a kind of rabbit and a tortoise was another name for a turtle. Anyway, in the fable, the hare kept playing and hopping back and forth, but the tortoise kept on walking along very slowly. And when they came to the finishing line, the tortoise had won after all, because he hadn't stopped to hop, skip and jump.

When she got home Kate put fresh water in the turtle bowl on her new desk and shook a tiny bit of food on

top. Then she kicked off her shoes and wiggled her socks on the rug. It felt good. She put her chin on her hands and watched the turtles and admired the pretty yellow lines on their heads and their darling little webbed feet with five tiny claws.

"I wonder," she thought, "if they would like to have a race."

Gently Kate put the turtles side by side on the desk. They pulled in their feet and stayed perfectly still. Suddenly the little one thrust his head from his shell. He turned it this way and that, and Kate could see the throbbing in his throat as he breathed. He blinked. How very funny, she thought. He blinks *up* instead of down. She stared at his shiny beady eyes and sure enough he blinked up. She hopped up and went to the mirror, and holding one eye open with her finger, she blinked with the other just to make sure that little girls blink down even if turtles blink up. She went back and saw that the turtles were in the same spot. Then the big one put his head out and then his feet and fin-

ally his tail, and he started to walk, first to the right, then to the left. The little one didn't move at all.

Just then there was a loud knock at the door. "Davy!" called Kate and rushed toward the door. She went so fast that she stubbed her toe—she had forgotten that her shoes were off. It hurt, so she hopped the rest of the way.

Davy looked surprised. "Why are you hopping?" he asked

"Oh, never mind," said Kate. "Come see my turtles." She stopped hopping and ran ahead to her room.

"Here they are," she said, and her mouth stayed wide open after the last word.

"I thought there were two," said Davy, looking at one small turtle on the desk.

"There were," said Kate. "There

really were. They were going to have a race like the hare and the tortoise. But one of them is gone."

"Which one?" asked Davy. "What's his name?"

Kate felt tears coming to her eyes and yelled at Davy, "The littlest one, with the greenest back. I don't know them well enough to give them names and anyway turtles don't *need* names. It's the littlest one."

"Well," said Davy, "let's start looking. For instance your desk drawer is partly open and he might have fallen into it."

They pulled the drawer all the way out. They didn't have to look very long to know the turtle wasn't there.

"Maybe he fell behind the desk," said Davy. They looked there. No sign of a turtle. Kate started to cry.

"Look," said Davy. The big turtle was walking across the desk very fast. "He's racing," sobbed Kate, "but he has nobody to race with." She picked him up and put him in the bowl for safekeeping.

"Maybe he fell over this edge." They looked all around the floor but there was no turtle to be seen.

"If you were a turtle, Kate, where do you think you would go?" asked Davy.

Kate tried to stop crying so she could feel like a turtle, but it was pretty hard. Then she said, "I'd go somewhere dark and warm."

"Like under your sweater, maybe," said Davy and picked up Kate's sweater from the floor. But no—he wasn't under the sweater. They looked under the bed, where it was dark and cozy, and in the closet, but there was no turtle. Now Kate started to cry again. "If I hadn't rushed to the door I would have watched him," Kate said between sobs. "Now I've lost my turtle. And he isn't in back of the desk, and he isn't in front and he isn't anywhere else and he's probably dead."

Mother came in with Kenneth to see what had happened. Ken saw Kate in tears. "Don't cry," he said, and put his arms around her. "Look at me. I will be a turtle for you." He flopped down on the floor and tried very hard to pull his head and his hands into his turtleneck sweater. Then he swam on the floor.

"Here's your shoe, Kate," he said, and pulled it from way underneath the desk. "Don't cry."

Kate kicked the shoe away. It landed upside down next to her sweater.

"Let me help you look," said mother. She hunted everywhere but she didn't find the turtle.

Then Davy yelled, "Look!" He pointed at Kate's shoe in the middle of the floor. It was moving on one side.

Mother, Kate, Davy, and Kenny stared at that moving shoe. A tiny foot stuck out and then a little striped face. Out crawled the littlest turtle and stood still with his head stretched out. He looked at all of them. Then he started to walk as fast as he could straight towards Kate.

Muggsy

by Marion Holland

Mr. and Mrs. Butterfield got Muggsy at the pet store. They got cans of dog food, too, for Muggsy to eat.

Then they took Muggsy home to live with them.

But Muggsy found things pretty slow at the Butterfields' house. The Butterfields did not know how to do any of the things Muggsy liked to do. They did not know how to run or jump or play. They did not know how to throw a stick for Muggsy to run after.

The very first day Muggsy found a good stick and took it to Mr. Butterfield. Mr. Butterfield did not know what to do with the stick. He just looked at it. All he said was, "Well, well, well."

Mrs. Butterfield just looked at it, too. She said, "Oh dear. How did this big stick get in our yard?" She took the stick away, and Muggsy could not find it again.

Then the paper boy came in the yard and threw the paper at the house. Muggsy thought he had found a friend. If the paper boy could throw a paper, he could throw a stick, too.

Muggsy was so happy he jumped up at the paper boy.

The paper boy took one look at Muggsy's big ugly face, and he ran out of the yard as fast as he could go. He took papers to all the other houses on

Muggsy's street. At every house the paper boy said, "Look out for the ugly dog in the Butterfields' yard!"

The next day the paper boy just threw the paper in from the street. He did not come in Muggsy's yard at all.

After this, Muggsy stopped trying to play. He stopped eating, too. All day and every day Muggsy just did nothing.

Every night Mrs. Butterfield opened a big red can of dog food and put Muggsy's dinner down for him. "Come, Muggsy!" she called. "Eat your good dinner."

Every night Muggsy just looked at his dinner.

Mrs. Butterfield said, "Maybe Muggsy does not like the dog food in the red cans."

She went to the store and looked for some other dog food for Muggsy. She found dog food in blue cans and yellow cans and green cans. She took cans and *cans* and CANS and CANS of dog food home for Muggsy to try.

But Muggsy did not want any of them.

At last Mr. Butterfield said, "I know what to do. When I get home from work, I will take Muggsy out for a good fast walk. Then he will eat his dinner."

So every night, as soon as he got home from work, Mr. Butterfield called Muggsy. Then Muggsy and Mr. Butterfield took a good fast walk.

The boys and girls who were out playing took one look at Muggsy's big ugly face. They heard him huff and puff, and snort. They all ran away from him as fast as they could.

Muggsy and Mr. Butterfield walked up the street and down the street. Some nights they walked all over town.

When it was dinner time, Mr. Butterfield said, "Home, Muggsy. Time to go home."

Then they walked back home again.

And after a good fast walk Mr.

Butterfield sat down and ate a good big dinner.

But not Muggsy. He did not want a good big dinner. He did not want any dinner at all.

Benny lived on the street next to Muggsy's street. He did not know Muggsy.

One morning Benny went out to play, and he could not find any of his friends. It was the first day of school, and all of his friends were at school.

But Benny did not know this. He began looking for some friends to play with. He walked along his street, looking in all the yards. Then he went over to the next street and walked along it, looking in all the yards.

Benny came to Muggsy's yard. He looked in, and there was Muggsy.

"Hello, dog," said Benny.

Muggsy looked out at Benny.

"Hello, dog," said Benny again. "Can you come out and play with me?"

Muggsy came out of his yard so fast he bumped into Benny, and Benny fell down. But Benny just laughed.

He got up again and said, "Come on, dog. Let's go for a walk."

The first thing Muggsy did was find a stick for Benny to throw. Benny threw the stick, and Muggsy ran after it and took it back to Benny. Then Benny threw it again, and Muggsy ran after it again.

They did this over and *over* and OVER and OVER again.

It was fun. And all the time they walked and walked and ran and ran. At last Benny began to slow up a little. He looked all around. He did not know where he was.

Benny sat down and began to cry.

Muggsy was surprised. He did not know what Benny wanted.

He found a stick for Benny. But Benny did not want a stick. He just wanted to go home, but he did not know where home was.

"I want to go home!" said Benny.

Oh! Go *home*—this was what Mr. Butterfield said when it was time to go home.

Muggsy began to go home.

He looked back. Benny was not coming.

Muggsy went back and pushed Benny. He made Benny get up. Then he pushed him again and made Benny walk along with him.

Muggsy took Benny home. Home to Muggsy's house.

Muggsy walked in the yard, and Benny walked in, too. Muggsy pushed the door open and walked in the house. Benny walked in, too.

Mrs. Butterfield looked up, and there was Benny.

"Where do you live, little boy?" asked Mrs. Butterfield.

Benny said, "Now I know where I live. I can find my house from here."

So he went out to look for his house, and Muggsy and Mrs. Butterfield went with him.

As soon as Benny found his house, he called to his mother, "Mother! Look! I found a friend! Come out and see what he can do!"

Benny's mother came out, and Benny got a stick and threw it for Muggsy. Muggsy ran after it and took it back to Benny. Then Benny threw it again, and Muggsy ran after it again.

Mrs. Butterfield was surprised. "So this is what Muggsy wanted!" said Mrs. Butterfield. "All this time he just wanted a friend to play with!" So she asked Benny's mother if he could come over to Muggsy's house in the morning and play with Muggsy. Benny's mother said yes.

Benny said to Muggsy, "See you in the morning."

Then Mrs. Butterfield took Muggsy home. She opened a can of dog food and put it down for Muggsy, and Muggsy ate it all up, very fast.

Every morning after that Benny went over to Muggsy's house to play.

When school let out, all the other boys and girls saw Benny in Muggsy's yard playing with Muggsy. So they all wanted to play with Muggsy, too.

The paper boy came and threw sticks for Muggsy, and he was very good at it. The big boys let Muggsy come and play ball with them, and Muggsy was just fine at playing ball.

Pretty soon Muggsy had friends all over town.

Every night now Mr. Butterfield calls Muggsy, and they go for a walk.

Muggsy has friends on every street.

When they see Muggsy, they all come running. Muggsy has to stop so his friends can talk to him and throw things for him.

Now Muggsy and Mr. Butterfield cannot take good fast walks. They take slow walks.

And when they get home, Mr. Butterfield does not want to eat a good big dinner.

But Muggsy does!

Every night Mr. Butterfield says, "Just look at Muggsy eat! He is eating us out of house and home."

But Mr. Butterfield is just talking, and Muggsy knows it.

After all, Mrs. Butterfield has all that dog food from the store. Cans and *cans* and CANS and CANS of dog food!

And Muggsy is eating it every day.

He is very happy.

Where's Willie?

by Seymour Reit

Willie was a kitten. He had big blue eyes and a small pink nose. And he had a boy of his own, named Peter.

When Willie came to stay, Peter's father gave him a fine straw basket with a big soft pillow.

He said, "This is for Willie to sit in." But Willie never did.

Willie had no time to sit. He was too busy sniffing and snooping and poking and pawing and running and rolling and crawling into things.

Willie liked crawling into things best of all.

He crawled into bags and boxes. He crawled into pans and pails.

He crawled into socks and sacks. He crawled into hats and holes.

Willie crawled into everything that could be crawled into.

But Willie never crawled into his straw basket with the big soft pillow.

One day Willie was gone.

Peter looked and looked, but he couldn't find his kitten anywhere. Soon the phone rang. It was the postman. He said, "I found Willie in my mailbag. Do you want me to mail him someplace?"

Peter's father said, "No. We will come and get him."

So he and Peter went to the post office and brought Willie home.

The next day, Willie was gone again. Peter looked and looked, but he couldn't find his kitten anywhere.

Soon the phone rang. It was the grocer. He said, "I found Willie in my grocery basket. Do you want me to put him on the shelf and sell him?"

Peter's father said, "No. We will come and get him."

So he and Peter went to the grocery store and brought Willie home.

The next day, Willie was gone AGAIN.

Peter looked and looked, but he couldn't find his kitten anywhere.

Soon the phone rang. It was the laundryman. He said, "I found Willie in my laundry bag. Do you want me to wash and iron him?"

Peter's father said, "No. We will come and get him." So he and Peter went to the laundry and brought Willie home.

Every day, Peter and his father went to get Willie.

And every day, Willie went right on crawling into things.

But Willie never crawled into his

straw basket with the big soft pillow.

One day, Willie was gone for a long time.

Peter waited for the phone to ring. He waited and waited and waited and waited.

But it didn't ring at all!

Peter began to worry.

He phoned the postman, but Willie wasn't there.

The postman began to worry.

He phoned the grocer, but Willie wasn't there.

The grocer began to worry.

He phoned the laundryman, but Willie wasn't there.

Soon, everybody was looking for Willie.

The laundryman phoned the milkman.

The milkman phoned the painter.

The painter phoned the plumber.

The plumber phoned his Uncle Fred.

His Uncle Fred phoned the lady next door.

The lady next door phoned the man across the street.

They looked and looked and looked, but they couldn't find Willie anywhere.

Peter looked the hardest of all.

He looked in all the bags and boxes.

He looked in all the pans and pails.

He looked in all the socks and sacks.

He looked in all the hats and holes.

But he couldn't find Willie anywhere.

Peter was very sad. He said, "We will NEVER find Willie. This time he is gone for good."

Just then, Peter heard a noise. He ran into the next room.

THERE WAS WILLIE!

Willie was sitting in the middle of his straw basket, right on the big soft pillow!

And he liked it!

The Dog Who Came to Dinner

by Sydney Taylor

Mr. Brown looked at the empty house next door.

"That house has been empty for a long time," he said.

"Yes," said Mrs. Brown.

"And it is such a nice house, too. I wish some nice family would move into it."

"A family with a girl," said Jane.

"A family with a boy," said Jimmy.

But no one moved in.

One day the Brown family went on a trip. When they came home, Mr. Brown cried, "Look! There is a new mailbox on the fence next door!"

Jimmy ran to look. "The name on the box is Lane!"

"Oh how nice!" said Mrs. Brown. "Someone has moved into the empty house!"

"We must make them feel at home," said Mr. Brown.

"Yes," said Mrs. Brown. "I will ask them to come to our house for dinner."

That night when Mr. Brown opened the door—in came Mr. and Mrs. Lane. In came Peter and Peggy Lane. And IN CAME A BIG DOG!

"How do you do?" said Mr. Brown.

"How do you do?" said Mr. and Mrs. Lane.

"It was nice of you to ask us to dinner."

"We are glad to have you," said Mrs. Brown. "Dinner will be ready soon."

They all went into the living room and sat down.

Mr. and Mrs. Brown talked to Mr. and Mrs. Lane. Jimmy Brown talked to Peter Lane. Jane Brown talked to Peggy Lane.

The big dog ran round and round the room. He ran to Mr. Brown. "Ark! Ark!" he barked.

Mr. Brown patted him. "Nice dog," he said.

The dog ran to Mrs. Brown. He put his front paws in her lap. "Oh!" cried Mrs. Brown, laughing.

Then the dog ran to Mrs. Lane. He wagged his tail. Mrs. Lane patted him.

"Nice dog," she said.

Next the dog ran to Mr. Lane. He sniffed at Mr. Lane's shoes. Then he chewed on the shoes. Mr. Lane pulled his feet away.

Now the dog ran to Jane. He tried to jump into her lap. His wet tongue licked her face. Jane laughed.

Peggy tried to stand up. The dog jumped up to lick her face too. Peggy fell down on top of Jane. Everyone laughed.

The big dog seemed to be laughing, too. He ran round and round and tried to catch his tail.

Soon he ran to Peter and Jimmy. He jumped all over them and licked their faces.

"He likes to play," said Peter.

"Yes," Jimmy said.

"See how his tail is wagging."

Now the dog smelled something nice. He poked his nose into the candy dish. Crunch! He chewed some candy. Crunch! Crunch! He chewed some more candy.

He ran to another nice smell. He poked his nose into the cookie dish. Crunch! He chewed on a cookie. Crunch! Crunch! He chewed on some more cookies.

The children laughed. "He likes sweets!" they cried.

Mr. and Mrs. Brown did not like it. They looked at Mr. and Mrs. Lane. But they did not say anything. They were too polite.

Mr. and Mrs. Lane looked at Mr. and Mrs. Brown. But they did not say anything.

Then Mrs. Brown said, "Dinner is ready."

They all went into the dining room and sat down.

The big dog went into the dining room, too. But he did not sit down. He ran round and round the room.

He put his front paws on the table and sniffed at Mr. Lane's plate. He poked his nose into Mrs. Lane's plate. His wet tongue washed Jane's plate. His front paws went all over Jimmy's

plate. He wagged his tail. Mr. and Mrs. Brown did not like it. They looked at Mr. and Mrs. Lane. But they did not say anything. They were too polite. Mr. and Mrs. Lane did not tell the dog to stop. They looked at Mr. and Mrs. Brown. But they did not say anything.

Then Mr. Brown said very politely, "What is the name of your dog?"

"Our dog?" said Mr. Lane.

"He is not our dog!" cried Mrs. Lane.

"Oh!" said Mr. and Mrs. Brown.

"But he came in with you!" Jane said.

"He was standing in front of your house," Peter said.

"So we thought he was your dog!" cried Peggy.

"Our dog?" said Mr. Brown.

"He is not our dog!" cried Mrs. Brown.

"Oh!" said Mr. and Mrs. Lane.

Then Mrs. Brown said, "He is not your dog. He is not our dog. Whose dog is he?"

"He must belong to someone!" Jimmy cried. "He has a collar."

Mr. Brown looked at the collar. "He lives on the next block."

"Why did he come to our house?" asked Jane.

"He wants to make some new friends, too," said Mrs. Lane.

"So he came to dinner," said Mrs. Brown.

Everyone laughed and laughed. The dog barked and wagged his tail.

"The dog poked his nose into all our plates," said Mrs. Brown. "Come Jane, we must wash them. Then we will have our dinner."

"And the dog, too?" cried the children.

"Yes," said Mr. Brown. "The dog will have some dinner, too."

When dinner was over, they all went into the living room and sat down.

"It was such a nice dinner, Mrs. Brown," said Mrs. Lane.

"I am glad you liked it," said Mrs. Brown.

"Ark! Ark!" barked the dog.

"He liked the dinner, too," said Peggy.

"Yes," said Peter. "See how his tail is wagging."

The dog ran to the door. He put his front paws on it. "Ark! Ark!" he barked.

Jimmy said, "Dinner is over. Now he wants to go home."

Everyone laughed and laughed. The dog seemed to be laughing, too. He barked again and wagged his tail.

Mr. Brown opened the door.

The dog who came to dinner ran all the way home.

Henry

by Elizabeth Vreeken

It was Judy's birthday. She got many cards.

One card was very heavy. It had ten dimes on it.

The card said, "Buy something you want. With love, Aunt Ann."

Judy did not know what to buy.

"You can buy a red hat," said Mother.

"A game is more fun," said her brother Mike.

Judy did not want a hat. She did not want a game.

"I think I will go down to Joe's Pet Shop," said Judy.

"Not another pet!" said Father.

Judy went down to see Joe in the pet shop.

When Judy came home, she had a box in her hand. In the box was a little ball of white fur. It was a little white mouse!

"What is your little mouse's name?" asked Mother.

"Henry is his name," said Judy.

"That box is too little for Henry," Mike said.

"He wants more room to run around," said Mother.

"I will make a house for him," said Mike.

Mike got a big box. He put a screen on the sides and on top. He put some sawdust on the floor. He made a little door.

Then Mike made a sign and hung it on the door. It said, "Mouse House."

Judy took Henry out of the little box. She put him in his little house.

"Do you like your house, Henry?" asked Judy.

Henry did not answer. He was running around his little house.

"Henry likes his house," said Mother. "Maybe he would like something to eat."

"What can he eat?" asked Mike.

Judy said, "Joe told me what Henry can eat. He can have bird seed and a little bread soaked in water. He can have a little nut or little pieces of vegetables."

Judy put a little box in Henry's house for a bed. She put some soft white cotton on it.

Mike made a water fountain for Henry. He made it with a little bottle and a tube. He hung the bottle upside down.

"Henry can have water any time he wants it," said Mike.

Henry liked the little house Mike made. Henry had fun in his house. He ran around in the sawdust on the floor.

He drank from his fountain. He had something to eat any time he wanted it.

And when he was tired, he went to sleep in his soft bed.

Henry liked Mike and Judy too.

Judy taught Henry a trick. She taught him to eat from her hand.

Judy taught her little white mouse another trick. When she put food in his house, she rang a bell.

Soon Henry knew what the bell was for. When Judy rang the bell, Henry came running.

Then Mike taught Henry a trick too.

He put a little nut in one of his pockets. Henry sniffed and sniffed. Then he ran up into Mike's pocket to get the nut.

After that Henry always knew where to get a nut.

One Sunday Mother was making pancakes. She put some batter in a pan. Some of the batter made a very little pancake.

"That one is for Henry," said Father.

Judy went to Henry's house. She rang Henry's bell. Henry came running. He took the pancake from Judy's hand. He sat up and began to eat it.

After that, Henry had a little pancake every Sunday.

One day Father said, "Next Sunday we are going away. Who will take care of Judy's pets?"

"I will take one pet," said Grandmother. "But I do not want to take care of the mouse. I do not like mice!"

"I will take one pet," said Aunt Ann. "But I do not want to take care of the mouse. I am afraid of mice!"

"I will take a pet," said the lady next door. "But I do not want to take care of the mouse."

No one wanted to take care of Henry!

"We can ask Joe in the pet shop," said Mike to Judy.

They ran to the pet shop.

"I do not have room for his house," said Joe. "I will put him with the other mice."

"How will I know which one is Henry? They all look alike!" said Judy.

"We can put a piece of red string on his leg," said Mike.

"Then you will know which one is Henry," Joe said.

Everyone was happy. The family went away.

When Judy came back, she ran to the pet shop. She looked and looked. She looked at every mouse. Not one had a red string on his leg.

"Where is Henry?" asked Judy. "I do not see any mouse with a red string on his leg!"

"He took it off," said Joe. "He did not like it."

"How will I know which one is Henry?" asked Judy.

"You can have any mouse," said Joe. "They are all the same."

"Oh, no," said Judy. "They are not all the same. I want Henry."

When Judy told her family, they were all very sad.

Then Judy said, "I will get the bell. Maybe Henry will remember the bell."

"And I will make a very little pancake," said Mother.

Mike and Judy went back to the pet shop.

When Judy rang the bell, the mice were afraid. They ran to hide.

All but one little mouse! He sat up. He sniffed and sniffed.

Mike opened the door. He rang the bell. The little mouse came running. He took the pancake from Judy. He sat up and began to eat it.

Mike took the little mouse in his hand. He ran up into Mike's pocket.

"It is Henry!" said Mike. "He is looking for his nut."

Henry went home in Mike's pocket. Soon he was in his little house. Everyone was happy.

"Next time we go away we will have to get a baby sitter," said Father.

"Not a baby sitter," said Mother. "A mouse sitter!"

Peppermint

by Dorothy Grider

Once there was a cat named Candy. She was called Candy because she lived in Mr. Dobby's candy store.

One day Candy had four little kittens in her basket beside the stove.

When Mr. Dobby saw the little kittens, he gave each one of them a candy name.

The tan and white kitten he named Lollipop.

The black and white one was called Chocolate Drop.

The tan one with the white face was Caramel.

And there was little Peppermint, who was all white and very thin.

Peppermint was not as beautiful as Lollipop and Chocolate Drop and Caramel.

After school, when the children came to the store to buy candy, they said "Oh!" and "Ah!" when they saw Lollipop and Chocolate Drop and Caramel. But when they saw poor little Peppermint, they said, "Oh my, isn't the little white one thin? Is she sick, Mr. Dobby?"

Mr. Dobby liked all of his cats, but he was too busy to take care of so many pets. Candy was a great help in chasing the mice away, so she would stay at the store. But the kittens would have to find other homes.

Mr. Dobby had a big sign made. He put the sign in his window.

KITTENS
FOR SALE
15¢

Mr. Dobby was a wise man. He knew how much little boys and girls like candy. He knew that if they spent their candy money for a kitten they would be kind and gentle to it.

Lollipop was the first kitten to go. A little girl in a red coat came first. She was very happy to carry Lollipop home.

Next came a little boy with fifteen pennies held tightly in his handkerchief. He couldn't decide between Chocolate Drop and Caramel. Finally he carried the black and white kitten away.

Now only Candy and Caramel and Peppermint were left.

Late the same afternoon a little boy

and girl left their wagon at the door and came into the candy store.

"We'd like a kitten, sir," the little boy said.

In a few minutes Caramel rode away in the wagon with her two new owners.

That left Peppermint all alone with Candy and Mr. Dobby.

Days went by. No one offered to buy the little white kitten, so Mr. Dobby took the sign out of the store window.

It was not many days before Peppermint's fur was a dirty gray, because she spent so much of her time in the storeroom hiding behind boxes and barrels.

One afternoon the children rushed into the candy store. They were all excited as they told Mr. Dobby about the big Cat Show they were going to have at school. Caramel, Chocolate Drop, and Lollipop were all going to be there.

The children soon ran home to get their kittens ready. But one little girl in a worn-out sweater stayed behind. She was rubbing her eyes and looking very sad.

"What's your name, little girl?" Mr. Dobby asked.

"Barbara," said the little girl.

"What is the matter, Barbara?" Mr. Dobby asked. He didn't like to see little boys and girls unhappy.

"I—I haven't a kitten," Barbara sobbed.

"Dear me," said Mr. Dobby.

He had grown very fond of Peppermint. But when he saw how unhappy Barbara was, he said, "You may have Peppermint."

Barbara was too happy to speak. She picked up Peppermint and held her close. "Thank you, Mr. Dobby," she

said, and she ran all the way home to her mother.

Barbara's mother was washing clothes. She stopped to hear all about the Cat Show and Mr. Dobby and Peppermint.

"We'll have to give Peppermint a bath," Barbara's mother said when she saw the soiled white cat. "She'll never win a prize looking like this."

She took the dirty little kitten and put her in the tub of soapy water.

Peppermint didn't like having a bath. She jumped out of the tub—right into a pan of bluing.

Barbara started to cry. She knew Peppermint was ruined. But her mother caught the kitten, wrapped her in a towel, and put her in the sun to dry.

The next morning Barbara's mother tied a big pink ribbon around Peppermint's neck. She put her in a basket so Barbara could carry her to school.

When Barbara reached school all the other boys and girls were proudly hold-

ing their kittens. They wondered what Barbara had in her basket.

One by one the children took their kittens to the front of the room. Finally it was Barbara's turn. Carefully she took Peppermint from the basket and held her up for all the children to see. How surprised they were!

Peppermint was no longer a soiled white kitten. Now she was a beautiful, fluffy, blue kitten with a pink bow around her neck.

"Oh!" said some of the children.

"She's beautiful!" said others.

"She should have first prize," someone else said.

So Peppermint did win first prize at the Cat Show.

She was the happiest kitten in the schoolroom. And Barbara was the happiest little girl.

Gallons of Guppies

by Beverly Cleary

Henry liked to go to the pet store. The windows were full of puppies and kittens and, just before Easter, rabbits and baby chicks and ducks. Inside there was usually a parrot or a monkey, and once there had been a deodorized skunk. Henry thought it would be fun to have a skunk following him around, but when he found it cost forty dollars he gave up the idea.

Best of all Henry liked the fish. One side of the store was covered with rows of little tanks. Each aquarium contained green plants that grew under water, snails, and a different kind of tropical fish. Henry always stopped to look into each tank. He liked the dollar-sized, black-and-silver-striped angelfish and the inch-long orange moonfish with their velvety fins and tails. He thought the tiny catfish were fun to watch, because they stayed on the bottom of the tanks, rolled their eyes, and used their whisker-like barbels to feel around in the sand for food. Mr. Pennycuff, who owned the pet store, explained that the

fish came from all over the world, but most of them came from jungle rivers where the water was warm. That was why they were called tropical fish.

One Friday when Henry went to the pet store he saw a sign that read:

SPECIAL OFFER
1 PAIR OF GUPPIES
FISH BOWL
1 SNAIL
AQUATIC PLANT
PACKAGE OF FISH FOOD
All for 79¢

"Jeepers!" said Henry. "All that for seventy-nine cents!" He looked at the fish in the bowls. Each bowl held one plain silvery-gray fish almost two inches long and one smaller fish with all the colors of the rainbow. "That really is a bargain!"

"It certainly is," agreed Mr. Pennycuff. "Shall I wrap up a pair for you?"

Henry felt around in his pocket. The dollar his grandfather had given him was still there. He watched the little rainbow fish chase the silvery fish and decided he had to have a pair of guppies. After all, it was his very own money he was spending. He would keep them on the dresser in his room. They would just stay in his room and swim quietly around in their bowl. He didn't see how his mother could object to two quiet little fish that didn't bark or track in mud or anything.

"I'll take a pair," Henry told Mr. Pennycuff, and watched him fasten waxed paper around the top of the bowl with a rubber band and put it into a bag.

"Now be sure to put the bowl near

a heater in cold weather so the fish won't get chilled and catch ick."

"Ick?" said Henry.

"Yes, ick. It's short for ichthyophthirius. When the fish get chilled, they catch ick and are covered with tiny white spots."

"Gosh," said Henry. Maybe there was more to keeping guppies than he thought.

"Oh, don't worry," said Mr. Pennycuff. "They can stand water down to sixty degrees. If it were that cold in the house, you'd have the heat on."

That sounded easy. "How often do I change the water?" asked Henry.

"You shouldn't have to change the water. The snails help keep it clean. Just give the fish a tiny pinch of food once a day. It's only when the fish don't eat all their food or when you have too many fish in a bowl that the water gets dirty." Mr. Pennycuff gave Henry his change.

"I didn't know that," said Henry. "I'm glad you told me."

When Henry returned with the fish to his house on Klickitat Street, he opened the door and yelled, "Hey, Mom! Come and see what I bought with the dollar Grandpa gave me."

"I'm afraid to look," answered his mother from the kitchen. "What is it this time?"

"Fish."

"Fish?" Mrs. Huggins sounded surprised. "Did you want me to cook it for dinner?"

Henry carried his package into the kitchen. "No, Mom, you don't understand. Not dead fish. Live fish swimming around in a bowl of water. They're called guppies."

"Guppies?"

"Yes. Just two little fish. I'll keep them on my dresser and they won't be any trouble at all. They were on sale at the pet shop. They were a bargain. See, Mom?" Henry gently lifted the fish bowl out of the bag.

Mrs. Huggins put down the potato she was peeling. "Why, Henry, what pretty little fish!"

"I thought you'd like them." Henry was pleased.

His mother bent closer to the fish bowl. "But, Henry, what are those little dark things in the water?"

"What little dark things?" Henry looked closer.

"Why, they're baby fish," Mrs. Huggins exclaimed. "There must be fifteen or twenty."

"Baby guppies!" Henry was delighted. "Look, Mom, did you ever see such teeny-weeny little fish? Golly, they're so little just about all you can see are their eyes and their tails."

Mrs. Huggins sighed. "Henry, I'm afraid they won't be teeny-weeny little fish very long. They'll grow and then what are you going to do with them?"

"I don't know. I'll ask Dad." Henry was worried. "Maybe he knows about baby guppies."

But when Mr. Huggins came home from work, Henry was disappointed to learn that he knew nothing about little guppies. "Why don't you get a book about guppies from the library?" he suggested.

Mrs. Huggins said there would be time before dinner, so Henry found his library card and ran all the way to the library.

"Hello, Henry," said the lady in the boys'-and-girls' room at the library. "Have you come for another book?"

"I want a book about guppies," Henry answered. "I have some baby guppies and I don't know how to take care of them."

The librarian found a book on hobbies with a chapter on fish, but it did not tell much about guppies. "Just a minute, Henry," she said. "Maybe there is something in the adult room." She returned with a thick book about tropical fish. It was full of colored pictures. "I'm sure this will help you," she said, "but I'm afraid it's too hard for you to read. I'll let you take it out on your card if you think your mother and father will help you with it."

"Sure, my dad will help me."

The librarian stamped the book on his card and Henry, proud to have a grown-up book stamped on his library card, ran home with it.

After dinner Mr. Huggins sat down to read the fish book while Henry went to his room to watch his guppies. This time he counted thirty-eight babies. After a while his father came in with the book in his hand. "This is a mighty interesting book, Henry, but you're going to need some more fish bowls. According to this book you can't keep so many fish in one bowl."

"But Dad, where will I get more bowls?"

"Maybe we can find something in the basement."

So Henry and his father rummaged through the basement until they found a gallon jar Mrs. Huggins used for making dill pickles.

"This should do," said Mr. Huggins. They carried it upstairs and washed it. Mr. Huggins filled it with hot water and carried it into Henry's room. "Now when the water cools we can move some of the little guppies. They can't live in cold water right out of the faucet. They need water that has stood or hot water that has cooled. While it's cooling, we can make a net." He found a piece of wire and bent it into a circle. Mrs. Huggins took an old stocking and sewed it to the wire to make a little fish net.

Henry and his father took turns catching the tiny fish with the net and moving them into the pickle jar. Henry was surprised that such small fish could swim so fast.

The next day and every day after

that Henry looked at his guppies the first thing in the morning. When he came home from school he looked at his guppies before he went into the kitchen for something to eat. His fish grew and grew. As the weeks passed the big guppies had more little guppies. The little guppies grew up to be big guppies and had little guppies of their own. Henry had hundreds of guppies. He couldn't find any more pickle jars so he started using his mother's quart fruit jars. He couldn't keep many fish in a quart of water.

Henry had jars on his dresser. He had them on the table by his bed. He put jars on the floor all around the edge of his room. When he had one row of jars all the way around the floor, he started another row.

"Goodness, Henry," his mother said, "pretty soon you won't be able to walk in here."

"If you keep all your guppies," said his father, "by the end of the year you'll have over a million fish in your bedroom!"

"Golly!" said Henry. "A million fish in my bedroom!" Wouldn't that be something to tell the kids at school!

Henry was glad when summer vacation started. It took him so long to feed his fish that he no longer had time to play with the other children on Klickitat Street. He spent all his allowance on fish food, snails, and plants for his jars. He slept with his window shut if he thought the night was going to be cold. He wasn't going to have his fish getting sick if he could help it.

All day long the boys and girls in the neighborhood rang the doorbell and asked to see Henry's fish.

Finally his mother said, "Henry, this can't go on. You must get rid of some of those fish. You'll have to give them to your friends."

Henry liked each fish so much he couldn't decide which one he liked best. They were all so lively, swimming around in their fruit jars. Henry didn't see how he could part with any of them, but now that he was on the third row of jars around his room, he decided to try. He started asking his friends if they would like some fish.

Scooter didn't think he had time to take care of fish. He delivered the *Shopping News* two days a week.

Mary Jane said her mother wouldn't let her have any fish. Mary Jane's mother was very particular.

Robert said he would rather come over and look at Henry's fish than take care of guppies of his own.

Finally Beezus said she would take one fish. Beezus' real name was Beatrice, but her little sister Ramona called her Beezus and now everyone else did too. Beezus and Ramona already had a cat, three white rats, and a turtle, so one fish wouldn't make much difference. It took Henry a long time to decide which guppy to give her.

Then one morning Mrs. Huggins came home from the supermarket with three lugs of apricots in the back seat of the car. When Henry helped her carry them into the house, she said, "Henry, run down to the basement and bring up about twenty quart jars. These apricots are so ripe I want to start canning them right away."

Henry went down to the basement. He did not come back with twenty quart jars. He came back with four. "These are all I could find, Mom," he said.

"Oh, dear, and one of them has a crack." Mrs. Huggins looked at the three lugs of apricots. Then she looked at Henry. "Henry," she said, and he knew from the way she said it she meant whatever she was going to say, "go to your room and bring me seventeen quart jars. And don't bring me any jars with guppies in them, either."

"Yes, Mom," said Henry in a meek

voice. He went into his room and looked at the jars of guppies. He guessed he did have too many fish. But they were such nice fish! He got down on his hands and knees to look at his pets.

"Henry!" his mother called. "I am starting to pit the apricots. You'll have to hurry!"

"O.K." Henry took his net and started catching the smallest guppies. The only thing he could do was to move them in with the other fish. He hated to do it, because the fish book said they shouldn't be crowded. When the guppies were moved, he carried the jars into the kitchen and poured the water down the sink.

"I'm sorry, Henry," his mother said, "but after all, I did tell you some time ago that you couldn't go on putting guppies in fruit jars."

"I know, Mom. I guess I'll have to think of something else." It took Henry the rest of the morning to feed his fish. He had to put the tiniest pinch of the finest fish food into each jar. He could hear Robert and Beezus playing cowboy in the vacant lot. Henry began to wish he were outdoors, too, but he couldn't let his little fish go hungry.

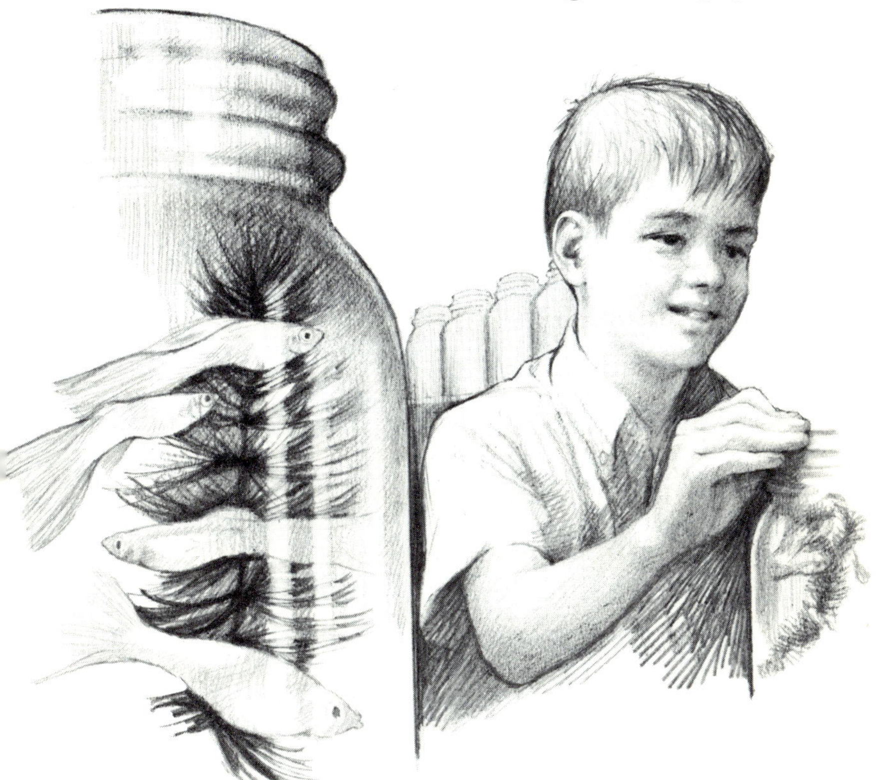

Late that afternoon Mrs. Huggins drove downtown to pick up Henry's father after work. When they returned, Henry saw his father carrying more lugs of apricots into the kitchen. He had a feeling he knew what was coming next.

It came.

"Henry," his mother said, "I am afraid I'll have to ask you for some more fruit jars."

Henry sighed. "I guess I'll have to double them up some more." He started to go to his room and then turned back. "Say, Mom, are you going to can anything besides apricots this year?"

"Yes, tomatoes and pears. And I thought we might go out to Mount Hood and pick huckleberries. You like huckleberry pie during the winter, don't you?"

Henry certainly did like huckleberry

pie. He liked it any time of year. He went to his room and moved more of his guppies. Tomatoes, pears, and huckleberries. He could see that his mother would need all her fruit jars before the summer was over. That would leave him his original bowl and the gallon pickle jar.

"Hey, Mom!" he yelled. "Are you going to make dill pickles, too?"

"Yes, Henry."

There went the pickle jar. By the end of the summer Henry would have to move the hundreds of fish he had now, and goodness knows how many more, back into the bowl. There would be so many fish, there wouldn't be room for any water.

That settled it. Henry decided he would have to get rid of all his guppies. He hated to do it, but if he kept even two he would soon be right back where he was now. It would be nice to have time to play outdoors again. Henry made up his mind to take every one of his fish back to the Lucky Dog Pet Shop. Maybe Mr. Pennycuff could have another sale.

Henry was chasing a guppy with the

net when his father came into the room. He told his father what he planned to do. "I sure hate to do it," he mourned, "but I can't keep a million guppies in my bedroom." He looked sorrowfully at his fish.

"I know, Henry. I hate to see the fish go, too, but they're getting out of hand. I'll tell you what to do. Catch all the guppies and put them into the pickle jar. It won't hurt them to be crowded for a little while. Right after supper I'll run you down to the pet shop in the car."

Henry sadly packed up his fish, and after supper he and his father got into the car and drove to the pet shop.

"I brought you a lot of guppies," Henry said to Mr. Pennycuff. "I hope you can use them."

"Use them!" exclaimed Mr. Pennycuff. "I certainly can. I haven't had a guppy in this store since the sale. Let's see them."

While Henry unwrapped his pickle jar, his father looked at the tanks of tropical fish along the wall.

"I should say you do have a lot of guppies," said Mr. Pennycuff. "Nice healthy ones, too. You must have taken good care of them." He held the jar up

to the light and looked at it closely. It seethed with gray guppies, rainbow guppies, and baby guppies of all sizes, swimming round and round. "Hmmmm. Let's see. We-e-ell." Mr. Pennycuff continued to stare at the fish.

Henry couldn't understand why he was muttering to himself that way. He had given Mr. Pennycuff the guppies and now he wished he would return the pickle jar so he could go.

"Well, now," said Mr. Pennycuff, "I guess these fish are worth about seven dollars. I can't give it to you in money, but you can pick out seven dollars' worth of anything in the store you want."

Seven dollars! Henry was astounded. Seven dollars' worth of anything in the pet shop! He was rich! He had been so busy thinking about getting rid of the guppies that it had not occurred to him they might be worth something to Mr. Pennycuff.

"Hey, Dad! Did you hear that? Seven dollars!" Henry shouted.

"I certainly did. You'd better start looking around."

"Take anything you want, sonny. Anything."

Henry tried to decide what he would like. He looked at the kittens. The sign read, "Kittens. One dollar each." They were cute, but Henry decided he didn't want seven dollars' worth of kittens.

"You don't have any skunks on sale for seven dollars?" he asked hopefully.

"No, I haven't had any skunks for a long time."

"I'm glad to hear that," said Mr. Huggins.

Henry looked at the tropical fish. Then he looked all around the store and came back to the tropical fish again. He stopped to watch a little catfish busily digging in the sand. Suddenly Henry knew that the only thing in the store he really wanted was more fish.

"Could I keep a catfish in my fish bowl?" he asked Mr. Pennycuff.

"No, sonny, they have to be kept in warm water. They need an electric heater and a thermostat in the water to keep the water the right temperature." He held up two long glass tubes. One looked as if it were filled with sand and the other with wires. "See, this is what I mean. They fit into the corners of an aquarium like this and keep the water warm all the time." He fitted them into the corner of a little tank on a table.

"How much does that cost?"

"The tank is three dollars and the heater and thermostat come to four. That makes seven dollars."

Henry was disappointed. "I wouldn't have any money left for a catfish, and the only thing I really want is more fish."

"You know, Henry, I hoped you'd say that," answered his father. "I hated to see those guppies go as much as you did. If you buy the tank and heater and thermostat, I'll buy the fish."

"Gee, Dad, that's swell! Let's get a little catfish!" Then Henry thought of something. "Do catfish have as many babies as guppies?" he asked Mr. Pennycuff.

"Oh my, no. Catfish rarely have babies when they're kept in tanks. They mostly have them when they live outdoors in ponds and rivers."

"Swell! said Henry. "That's the kind of fish we want. Won't Mom be surprised!"

Twenty-four Cakes of Flea Soap

by Carolyn Haywood

Billy knew that something was the matter. Daddy hadn't called him William since the day last spring when he broke the bathroom window with his baseball. He wondered, as he climbed the two flights of stairs, what he had done that would make Daddy call him William.

As he entered his daddy's room, he saw him standing over a large box.

"William!" said Daddy in a very stern voice, "do you know anything about this soap?"

"Soap?" said Billy.

"Yes. Soap," said Mr. Porter. "Flea soap. In fact, twenty-four cakes of flea soap. Two dollars and forty cents' worth of flea soap. Plus the worst smell in fifty states."

"Oh!" said Billy. "Oh! That's our soap."

"Our soap!" exclaimed Daddy. "What are we going to do with it?"

"No, Daddy," said Billy. "You don't understand. It belongs to our football team."

"Well, what I do understand is that I paid two dollars and forty cents for it," said Daddy. "So if it belongs to your football team, I would like to have the money returned to me." And then he added, "Promptly."

"Oh, sure, Daddy. Sure!" said Billy. "I'll call a meeting of the team tomorrow. And I'll bring the money home with me."

And with this Billy dashed for the head of the stairs.

"Hold on a minute," said his daddy. "What in the name of all smells does the team intend doing with this flea soap?"

Billy came back. "Why, we're going to sell it, Daddy, and get a football. We sell it for twenty cents a cake. Then we get the football."

"Well, get my two dollars and forty cents," said Mr. Porter. "And get rid of this soap as quickly as possible. I'll put it out in the garage. A gas mask should go with each cake."

The following day Billy met Betsy on the way to school.

"Hi, Betsy!" Billy called out. "Our soap has come."

"What soap?" said Betsy.

"Why, the flea soap that the team is going to sell to get the football," said Billy.

"Oh!" replied Betsy. "That soap!"

When the children reached the school, Billy sent word around that there would be a meeting of the football team at recess.

After the opening exercises Miss Pancake put some arithmetic problems on the blackboard and gave each child a piece of paper. Everyone set to work and the room was very quiet. In a few moments Sally, who sat across the aisle from Billy, looked up with a very strange expression on her face. She sniffed. And then she sniffed again.

In a few moments she tiptoed up to the front of the room and spoke to Miss Pancake in a very low voice.

Miss Pancake said, "Just sit here, at this table by the door."

Sally returned to her seat and got her paper. In a moment she was quietly working at the table by the door.

Very shortly Mary Lou, who sat across the aisle on the other side of Billy, raised her hand.

"What is it, Mary Lou?" asked Miss Pancake.

"May I please sit by the window?" said Mary Lou "I think I need a little more air."

"Certainly," replied Miss Pancake. And Mary Lou carried her paper over to the desk by the window.

In a few minutes Ellen, who was sitting behind Billy, raised her head from her work. She put her handkerchief to her nose and held it there while she did her problems.

When Miss Pancake looked at her, she said, "Is there anything the matter with your nose, Ellen?"

"I think maybe it would be better if I sat by the window too," replied Ellen.

"Very well," said Miss Pancake. And Ellen moved.

It wasn't long before Betty Jane, who sat in front of Billy, held up her hand.

"What is it, Betty Jane?" said Miss Pancake.

Betty Jane got up and walked up to the teacher's desk. She whispered something to Miss Pancake. Miss Pancake moved a chair over to the table beside Sally and Betty Jane sat down.

By this time Billy, who was busy working out his problems, looked like an island completely surrounded by empty seats.

Miss Pancake stood up and walked down the aisle. She stopped beside Billy's desk. She sniffed. Then she walked to the back of the room and up the other aisle. When she reached Billy's desk, she stopped again. Then she took out her handkerchief. She looked puzzled.

Just then Christopher looked up from his paper. He wrinkled up his nose and looked around. Then he said, "Gee, Miss Pancake! Something stinks!"

"Christopher!" said Miss Pancake. "I'm surprised at you. That is very vulgar."

"Well, it does, Miss Pancake," said Christopher. "It sure does st— I mean, smells awful. Worse than Limburger cheese."

By this time all of the children were sniffing. "Whew-ew!" they exclaimed.

"Be quiet, children," said Miss Pancake. "Does anyone know what this strange odor is?"

"Oh!" cried Billy, his face as bright as a dollar. "Maybe it's my soap. It's a new kind of flea soap, Miss Pancake. The football team is selling it. Only twenty cents a cake. It makes dogs happy."

"Well, perhaps," said Miss Pancake. "But it certainly is not making this room happy. So suppose you put the soap on the window sill outside the window."

"All right," said Billy.

"Say!" said Christopher. "I'm not going to sell anything that st— I mean, smells like that. Skunks!"

"Aw, the dogs will like it," said Billy.

Billy put the cake of soap on the

window sill and the little girls returned to their seats around Billy.

"Sissies!" said Billy. "That soap smells good. I would like to take a bath with it myself."

"Well, if you do I hope you'll take it Saturday night," said Ellen.

The soap sat on the window sill until recess. Then Billy took it and ran off to meet the football team.

Soon the boys were gathered together.

"The soap came," cried Billy as soon as his friend Rudy appeared. "I have a cake here. The rest of it is in our garage. My daddy paid for it."

"Gee! That's great!" interrupted Rudy. And the faces of the team lit up.

"But my daddy wants the two dollars and forty cents," said Billy. "So you'll have to collect the dues, Rudy."

The faces of the team grew long.

"O.K. O.K.," said Rudy. "Fellas, hand over your dues."

Eight hands went into eight pockets and all kinds of things came out. Marbles, screws, nails, bits of string, bottle tops, thumbtacks, rubber bands, bits of colored glass, pebbles, seashells, balls of tinfoil, golf balls, wheels from broken toys, and seventeen cents in all.

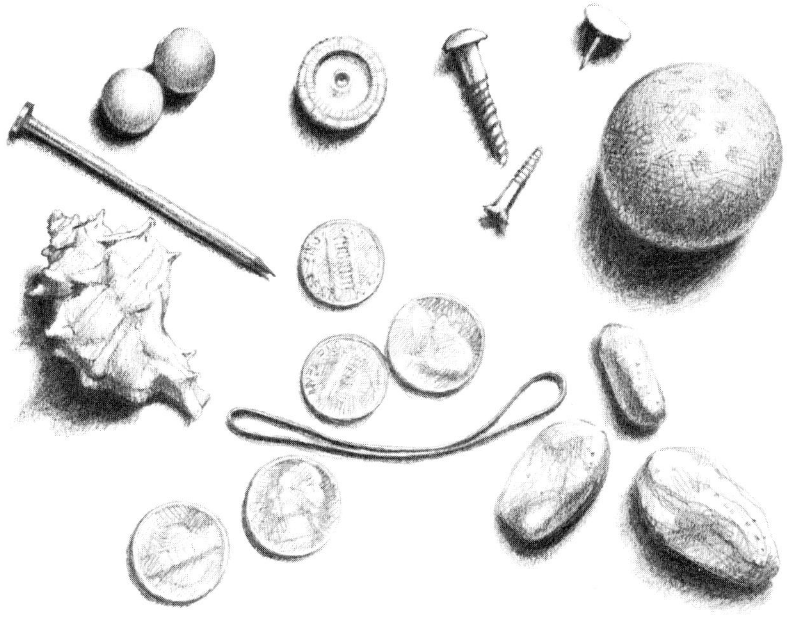

"Seventeen cents isn't enough," said Billy.

"Well, I don't think we can sell that soap anyway," said Christopher. "It st— you know."

"That's right," said Henry. And Richard, who was Henry's twin, said, "That's right."

"My father says I can't sell soap," said Kenny. "He says he won't allow it."

"Well, say! What am I going to do with all that soap, and what about my father's two dollars and forty cents?" said Billy. "What about that?"

"And what about our football?" said Rudy.

Just then little Eddie appeared. "Whatcha doin'?" said Eddie. "What's up?"

As usual nobody paid any attention to Eddie, so Eddie just hung around trying to pick up the news. It wasn't very long before he understood that Billy was stuck with two dollars and forty cents' worth of flea soap.

Nothing had been settled when the bell rang for the children to return to their classrooms. But it didn't look as though the boys were going to sell any soap.

Billy returned to his room looking very gloomy indeed. When Miss Pancake saw him, she said, "Goodness gracious, Billy! What is the matter?"

Billy told Miss Pancake the whole story about the soap.

"How many boys in the room are on the team?" said Miss Pancake.

A half dozen hands went up.

"Who is captain?" she said.

"Rudy Wilson," replied Billy.

"You boys stay after school for a

meeting," said Miss Pancake. "I'll send word to Rudy."

Rudy arrived as soon as the class was dismissed.

"Now," said Miss Pancake to the little boys, "you must work out a way to pay Billy's father the money that you owe him."

"But what about our football?" asked Rudy.

"Most of the boys tell me that they don't want to sell the soap," said Miss Pancake. "So you will have to get your football in some other way."

Just then little Eddie appeared in the open doorway "What's the matter?" asked Eddie.

"Are you on the team too?" asked Miss Pancake.

"Yes, ma'am," answered Eddie.

"No, he isn't," said Rudy.

"Am," said Eddie and sat down.

"Well now, boys, you will have to think of some way to raise the two dollars and forty cents. I'll write your ideas on the blackboard."

The team sat very still. They were all thinking hard.

Finally Eddie spoke up. "We could wash dogs," he said.

Miss Pancake wrote on the board, "Wash dogs."

"That is a very good idea," she said. "If you charge twenty-five cents each, how many dogs would you have to wash? Billy?"

"Ten," said Billy.

"That's an awful lot of dogs," said Rudy.

The boys sat still for five more minutes. Nothing was added to the blackboard.

At last Miss Pancake said, "Well, is this the only idea?"

The boys looked at each other. "Guess so," they murmured.

"All right!" said Miss Pancake. "Tomorrow is Saturday. You can all spend the day washing dogs."

"Where will we get the dogs?" asked Christopher.

"You will have to go out and find them," said Miss Pancake. "There must be plenty of people who would like to have their dog washed on Saturday morning."

"Where will we wash them?" asked Kenny.

"You will have to decide that," replied Miss Pancake.

"I guess we can wash them in our garage," said Billy. "That's where the soap is."

"Very well," said Miss Pancake. "You can go now, and on Monday morning I want to hear that your debt is paid and that every boy helped. And let this be a lesson to you, Billy. Never sign your name to anything you can't pay for."

"I'll remember, Miss Pancake," said Billy.

The following morning the boys

were up bright and early. They scoured the neighborhood for dogs to wash. By nine o'clock Billy was busy washing the next-door neighbors' Airedale.

He had just finished when Rudy arrived with a Scottie.

In the middle of the Scottie's bath Kenny came in with an Eskimo dog. Later Christopher brought in a fox terrier.

The dogs behaved very well. It was just as Billy had said. They liked the odor of the soap.

Late in the morning Richard and Henry arrived with their own red setter, Chummy. They set to work on him together.

Just as they finished Billy cried out, "Look what Eddie's bringing!" Billy pointed up the street. The boys looked. Then their mouths fell open. For there, moving majestically beside Eddie, was the biggest dog the boys had ever seen. It was a Saint Bernard.

"Take it away!" yelled Rudy.

"We're not washing that dog for twenty-five cents," called out Billy.

"Nix!" yelled Christopher. "Not for two bits."

Eddie was looking proud enough to burst. "The lady says she'll pay a dollar," said Eddie, waving a dollar bill.

"Oh, boy! Oh, boy!" cried Billy. "Bring him right in."

All the boys crowded around to pat the Saint Bernard dog. He was as good as gold. He stood still while Billy washed his big head and Rudy washed his back. Joe worked on his back legs and Kenny washed his front legs. It was a big job, but when the boys had finished, the Saint Bernard looked beautiful with his shining white and gold coat.

When Eddie and the dog departed, Billy said, "Oh, boy! Just one more dog and we can quit."

"Yeh!" said Rudy. "But we haven't any football." And when he said this the team looked very sad.

"Oh, well! Maybe we can wash more dogs next week and buy a football," said Billy.

Just then Betsy appeared. "Hello!" she said. "What are you doing?"

"We're in business," said Rudy. "We wash dogs. Only twenty-five cents."

"Yes," said Billy. "Just one more dog and we have enough money to pay my daddy for the soap."

"But we have to wash more next Saturday," sighed Rudy, "to earn money to buy a football."

"Oh!" said Betsy. "That's too bad." And she trotted off.

The boys sat down to rest.

Just as the Wilson twins were about to set off to find the last dog, Betsy appeared. She had Thumpy on a leash. "Here you are," she said. "It smells awful but you can wash him."

The boys just stared, but not at Thumpy. They were staring at the object under Betsy's arm. They couldn't

believe their eyes. For under Betsy's arm was a football!

She held it out to them. "Would you like to play with my football?" she said.

"Oh, Betsy!" cried Billy. "Do you mean it? Is it a real football?"

"Sure," said Betsy.

"Wheee!" cried the team.

"What a pal! What a pal!" cried Rudy, patting Betsy on the back. "You're on the team, Betsy. You're on the team."

Then he turned to the boys. "Come on, fellas," he said, "give her a cheer."

And they all cried, "Rah! Betsy! Rah! Rah! Rah! Betsy!"

And Billy rubbed Surething Flea Soap on Thumpy.

The Best Birthday

by Quail Hawkins

When Dick Lyon woke up early Christmas morning, the rain was beating hard against the windows. The faint sound of the foghorns on the bay told him this was going to be a foggy, wet holiday. But Dick did not mind. He had lived all his seven and a half years in San Francisco, and it always rained like this in the winter.

For a minute he lay cuddled in his warm bed. Then he remembered what day it was. Christmas! He scrambled out of bed and ran down the hall to the living room in his bare feet. There it was, the stocking he had hung up the night before. It was filled to overflowing now, instead of hanging limp and empty as he had left it. He took the stocking down and ran back to bed with it.

The house was still dark, and it was very early. Dick knew he could look at his stocking and play with the toys in it until it was time to get up. He could hardly wait. He began to wish his father and mother would wake up.

Though he listened hard, there was no stir in the next room. All he heard was the beat of the rain on the windows and the sad blare of the foghorns on the bay.

The present he wanted most was another guinea pig. He already had one.

He called her Annabella, which was his favorite name. She was small, soft, with the prettiest brown and grey markings on her white fur.

Dick was sure his father would get him the new guinea pig. He just had to have another guinea pig. It was a small animal. It wasn't as if he had asked for a big present like a horse or an elephant!

There was another present he was going to get, only for New Year's, not Christmas. He was going to get this present whether he wanted it or not. His parents were going to give him a new baby brother or sister. They told him it would be much more fun with a bigger family. Dick just didn't see how they could have more fun than they did, just the three of them.

Well, anyway, this Christmas would be just the same as always. After they opened their presents they would go across the bay to Grandmother's home in Berkeley for Christmas dinner. Dick always loved the trip across the bay.

They took the cable car, the ferry, and the train before they got there.

Christmas was the best day of all. How he wished it would start. At last he could not wait another minute. He crawled out of bed. He knocked lightly at his parents' bedroom door. There was no answer. He peeked inside the door to see if they were really asleep or only pretending. Their bed was empty! Where's my family?

Dick looked around the room in surprise. It was not tidy the way Mother usually left things. The bed was not made, and his parents' nightclothes were thrown on the bed. Across the room, the bassinet, waiting for the new baby, sat quiet and empty.

He hurried to the kitchen. Probably his mother and father were up early too!

He pushed open the kitchen door, calling, "Merry Christmas!"

Dick stopped in surprise. The light was on, and there was coffee on the stove. But there was no mother or father in the kitchen. Sitting beside the breakfast table was Mrs. Noggin, who came in to look after him when his family went out to dinner. Right now, he didn't like her at all! He wanted his family on Christmas. Where were they?

Mrs. Noggin looked at him. She kept on stirring her cup of coffee as she said quietly, "Merry Christmas to you." Dick didn't even hear her. He almost shouted at her, "Where's my mother and father?"

"There's no need to shout. They're down at the hospital getting the new baby."

"But the baby isn't coming till New Year's Day. My mother told me so!" Dick's blue eyes began to brim with tears, even if he was seven and a half years old.

"With babies you never can tell. This one decided to come now." Mrs. Noggin went on stirring her coffee. She put down the spoon and took a sip from the cup. "There's no need to be upset. Come on now, and sit down like a good boy and eat some breakfast. There's your orange juice. I'll get your cereal as soon as I finish this coffee."

"I don't want any breakfast," said Dick in a tiny voice.

"Of course you want your breakfast," said Mrs. Noggin, putting her cup down and getting up stiffly. "Seeing it's Christmas, I'll make you pancakes if you want."

Dick didn't want pancakes. He felt as if he were choking. How could his mother and father leave him on Christmas? How could they? He stood staring at the floor and didn't answer.

Mrs. Noggin began to look cross. "Sit down," she said firmly.

Dick sat down. He picked up his orange juice and sipped it. It didn't taste good. He could hardly swallow. "I guess I'm not hungry," he said to Mrs. Noggin.

Dick got up from the table and went back to his room. He saw his Christmas stocking lying on the unmade bed. He saw the toys he had played with just a few minutes ago. He thought he would never play with toys again. Nobody loved him. All his mother and father cared about was the new baby.

TOYOTA

Then he remembered his grandmother. Why, she loved him. She always said she wished she had a nice boy like him to live with her. That's what he'd do. He'd go to Berkeley to live with his grandmother. Right now! When his family came home with the new baby, they would be sorry they had left him!

It was a long way to Grandmother's, on the cable car, on the ferry and train, and then up the hill on foot. Dick had been there before many times, though never alone. He knew the way perfectly. It was easy.

He wondered if he had enough money. He picked up his Mexican clay piggy bank. If you shook it just so, sometimes the coins would slip out.

After a good deal of work he managed to pry out two dimes, one nickel, and two pennies. It cost only a nickel to ride on the cable car, and twenty-one cents to go on the ferry and train. He didn't need more because he wasn't coming back.

Quickly Dick pulled on his clothes laid out beside his bed. He remembered to wash his face, because Grandmother liked clean hands and face even more than Mother did. He brushed his hair, but the part was a little crooked. Mother usually did the part.

It had almost stopped raining, but there was a heavy fog outside. Everything dripped wetly. Dick ran to the closet. He pulled out his slicker, his rain hat, and his rubber boots. He put on his boots.

Just as he was about to go out the door, he remembered. He had better leave a note for his dad. He used one of his new crayons to print in big letters, "Gone to live at Grandma's" and put it on his father's bed.

He thought for a moment. Annabella! He could not leave her. He would

slip her into his shirt, and nobody on the ferry would even guess. He hurried down the long back steps to the tiny garden. There at the end was Annabella's hutch. He picked her up carefully and slipped her into his shirt. She settled down and went to sleep against Dick's warm waist. Dick picked up a handful of dry food and slid it into his pocket.

AYLOR
502
"I stop
at the
St. Francis"

There was a cable car waiting at the end of the line when Dick got there. He climbed up the step onto the long open seat. He looked at the gripman, who was leaning against the side of the tiny car. Dick fished in his pocket for his nickel.

"Merry Christmas," the man said, taking the money.

"Merry Christmas," Dick answered. He looked around the car. It was empty except for the gripman and the conductor.

"You're out early," the gripman said cheerfully to Dick as he started the car. "Where are you going in all this wet?"

"I'm going to my grandmother's. My mother is at the hospital getting a new baby, and my dad is with her. But my grandmother likes me."

"Sure, kid." The gripman laughed: "I guess your nose will be out of joint with the new baby." Dick didn't answer. He put his hand in his shirt and felt Annabella quietly resting against him.

The fog was lifting. The wind began to blow in gusts. The heavy, dark clouds looked as if they would drop their load of rain again at any minute.

On down the hill they clanged, past the tall hotels, past the big apartments filled with sleeping people.

Dick kicked his heels against the step to keep his legs warm. He would be glad to get to the ferry building. The trip was longer than he remembered. Maybe it was because he was alone. Annabella couldn't talk.

Here they were now, at the end of the line. "Have a good time at your grandmother's," laughed the gripman. "Eat lots of turkey for me."

"Sure," Dick answered as he hurried down the block to the ferry building with its tall clock tower.

As Dick went into the waiting room of the ferry building, the wind began to blow more than ever. The rain came down hard. He was glad to get inside. He sat down on the edge of one of the many long seats to wait.

The big sliding door opened. The few people waiting walked onto the fat, white boat that looked like a waterbug on the water. Dick ran down the gangway and through the doors that led inside the ferry.

When Dick took hold of one of the big doors to try to open it, a man in blue dungarees came up to him. "Look, sonny," he said, "the weather's too bad to go outside. You'd better just stand inside and watch."

Dick looked up into the man's face. "Are you the captain?" he asked.

"I'm just the deck hand," said the man.

Dick knelt on the long seat by the windows. The boat was still tied to the slip, but it bounced up and down. Suddenly a loud whistle shook the boat, and it started out of the slip into the rougher waters of the bay. Dick could feel the boat tremble as the engine throbbed and they moved. The waves grew stronger and stronger. The boat began to sway from side to side.

This seemed to upset Annabella. She pushed out of Dick's shirt and climbed up onto his shoulder. Together they watched the storm outside getting wilder and wilder.

There was a stir among the passengers. Dick could see that something was wrong. The boat had stopped moving ahead and was rocking badly. The whistle let off several loud blasts.

Dick slid first one way on the seat and

then the other. He hung onto Annabella. The wind outside was howling. The water was breaking in big waves over the forward deck.

Dick wished the boat would stop rocking. His stomach felt funny. He wished he knew what was the matter. It was very strange but very exciting. He pretended he was at sea. Would the engines start soon? Would they be rescued by another boat? Would they have to climb into the other boat in all these waves? Would the other boat pull them to shore?

The other passengers seemed frightened. The deck hand was saying, "Please be calm. Everything is all right. A tugboat is on its way to take us safely back to San Francisco."

He saw Dick sitting there. "See," said the deck hand, "see, this little boy isn't afraid, are you, sonny?"

Dick shook his head. He wasn't afraid. But he was excited. The deck hand said, "The captain says everybody is to go to the restaurant to have a cup of coffee with his compliments." Turning to Dick, he whispered, "Why don't you go first? Then maybe the others will follow."

"O.K.," said Dick, staggering to his feet. Holding Annabella tightly, Dick and the deck hand went into the restaurant. Several passengers followed. In a few minutes the others had crowded in. The waiters were busy trying to fill and pass coffee cups and not spill them. It was a hard job, as the ferryboat was still rolling. Soon the people began to laugh as they tried to balance the cups themselves.

A waiter plunked a cup of coffee beside Dick and one for the deck hand. "My mother doesn't let me drink coffee," Dick confided to the deck hand.

"I don't think she'd mind this time. Here's a lot of cream. And some sugar. That'll make it taste better." The deck hand hung onto Dick's cup while he poured the cream. Dick laughed. He began to feel hungry. "Could I have a doughnut, please?"

The waiter gave Dick a doughnut and offered them to the others. Dick tried to interest Annabella in a doughnut. She just nibbled at it. The other passengers watched Annabella.

Then the deck hand said to Dick, "Do you know any Christmas songs? Let's see if we can start some singing."

"I know 'Away in a Manger' and 'O Come All Ye Faithful,'" Dick answered, "but not all the verses."

"I don't either," said the deck hand, "but let's try."

Dick began in his clear high voice.

"'Away in a manger, no crib for his bed . . .' " The deck hand added his deep bass voice to Dick's soprano.

Another voice joined in, and then another and another. Soon everyone was singing.

While they were still singing, the captain walked in. "The tugboat is almost here. Another boat will take you to Berkeley. I'm sorry for the delay." He went over to speak to the deck hand. "You've got a mighty fine bunch of passengers," said the captain. "Most people would be frightened."

"Well," said the deck hand, smiling down at Dick, who was standing beside him, "this young man is really responsible. I'll bet he's never had such an exciting Christmas before."

"No, sir, I haven't!" Dick grinned at the captain.

The deck hand stood looking at Dick patting Annabella. "You didn't tell me how come you are all alone on Christmas Day. Where are your folks? Are they going to meet you?"

Dick looked up at the man. He had been gentle with Annabella. He had let Dick help him. Maybe he would understand.

"I'm going to my grandmother's—to live. My mother's gone to the hospital to get a baby sister or brother. My dad's gone too. They said they were going to get the baby for New Year's and it came now. They left me all alone. On Christmas too!" Dick began to feel sorrier and sorrier for himself. He gulped a little and looked at the boards on the deck so the deck hand wouldn't see his face.

"Did they leave you all alone?" asked the deck hand. "Wasn't there anybody in the house?"

"Mrs. Noggin was there," Dick admitted. "But she's not family. She just comes in when Mother goes out to dinner."

"Does Mrs. Noggin know where you are?" the man went on gently.

"Well, I left a letter on the bed for my dad when he came back," Dick answered. He wasn't so sure it was a good idea to go away without telling her.

"Of course you know your mother and dad will miss you."

"Oh no, they won't. All they talk about is the new baby. They won't care at all."

"Excuse me, sonny, but I've got to

stop those passengers from crowding around that door. Want to come over with me and help some more?"

"Sure," said Dick, but now the excitement was over, he felt sad again. Here he was, coming back to San Francisco. It wasn't as easy as he thought to get to his grandmother's.

He watched the little tug come up to the big, clumsy ferry.

The boat hit with such force Dick was knocked off his feet. Annabella was thrown from his shoulder. He picked himself up and looked around for Annabella. Where was she? Had she been hurt?

"Annabella, where are you?" Dick called as he looked for her. He was afraid someone might have stepped on her.

"Here she is," said his friend, the deck hand. He picked Annabella off the seat where she was cowering in a corner, squeaking with fright. Dick gathered her into his arms. He sat down and started comforting her.

The deck hand bent over Dick and touched Annabella's fur softly. "You didn't tell me what kind of an animal Annabella is," he said.

"She's a guinea pig. My dad was going to get me another one for a Christmas present. Annabella gets lonesome when I go to school, so I asked for another one."

"If you get the new guinea pig, you'll like it a lot, won't you?"

"Oh, I'll love the new guinea pig. I'd like to have lots of them, not just two."

"I suppose when you get the new guinea pig you won't like Annabella as much as you do now. After all, you've had her quite a while. You won't have much time for her now, will you?"

"Not have time for Annabella? Say, what's the big idea, anyway? I guess she's the nicest guinea pig there is. Why, look at her!" Dick held Annabella up to show her off. She certainly was a nice-looking guinea pig. "Huh! Not like Annabella? That's why I want another one, because I like Annabella so much."

"Well, you said your parents would stop loving you just because they have a new baby. Naturally I thought you would like the new guinea pig better than Annabella." The deck hand wasn't looking at Dick. He was stroking Annabella softly.

By this time the boat had been pulled into the dock. The deck hand hurried off and helped put the gangplank down. All the passengers left, but Dick didn't move. He stood quite still, patting Annabella.

In a minute or two the deck hand

came back. "This boat isn't going back to Berkeley, but if you run quickly you'll have time to make the other boat that's starting over. The storm's almost over. You'll get to your grandmother's in time for turkey."

Dick looked up at the deck hand. "I guess I'm not going to go to my grandmother's after all. I guess I'm going home. Annabella is getting tired. She's not used to traveling."

The deck hand patted Annabella. "She'll probably enjoy her dinner much better in her own hutch. I'll see you get on the streetcar if you like."

"Thanks," Dick said, cuddling Annabella back into his shirt. "I'll be all right."

But he didn't feel all right. He felt foolish and empty. How could he have thought his dad and mother would not love him? It was so silly. He didn't see how he could face them. What was he going to do?

He started slowly toward the big doors that led to the gangplank. He hung his head, looking down at the deck and softly stroking Annabella. He heard hurrying footsteps. He looked up to see his father running onto the boat. "Dad!" Dick started to run too.

His father caught him in his arms. "Oh, Dick, are you all right?"

"Oh yes, Dad. I'm O.K." Dick gulped hard to keep from crying. "Gee, I'm glad you're here."

"Dick, you mustn't scare us like this again."

"I won't, Dad," Dick answered. "I didn't mean to scare you."

"You should be very proud of your son, mister," said the deck hand. "He has more spunk than most grownups. He helped me keep the passengers from panic. I think Annabella helped too."

Dick looked down at his pet. She was squeaking softly. "Annabella doesn't feel well, Dad. We've got to get her home. I don't think she likes traveling."

The deck hand went on while Dick patted Annabella, "I hear you have a new addition to your family. If the baby is anything like this young man, you'll be very lucky."

"We are lucky. Thank you for your kindness to my son."

Dick looked up. "Dad, has the baby come?"

"Your little sister arrived this morning. I'll tell you all about it later. I think now we'd better get Annabella home. I think she has had enough traveling, myself. Besides, I have a surprise for you there. We haven't even unwrapped our gifts. Then we'll go see Mother and the baby for a few minutes. After we leave them we'll both go to Berkeley to have our Christmas dinner with Grandmother." They said good-by to the deck hand and hurried out to the street.

Because it was Christmas they took a cab. As it started up California Street,

Dick and his father both sat silent. Finally his father said, "Dick, I'm sorry you didn't understand about the baby. We didn't think you'd be awake so early. Your mother and I hated being away on Christmas, but the baby didn't wait. Your mother sent me home just as soon as possible. We didn't expect the baby to be born on Christmas any more than you did. I know Christmas isn't a very good time to be born. And the baby won't like it either, when she's big enough to know."

"Why, Dad, I think Christmas is the best time of all to be born. Anyway, our baby was born in a hospital, and we have room for her. She has a bassinet waiting for her at home. And a whole family too!"

"You're right, Dick. Of course Christmas is a good birthday. And you know we still love you just as much even if we have a new baby, don't you?"

"Sure, Dad, I know. I know you love me the same as I love Annabella. You wouldn't like a new baby better than you like me. And I wouldn't like a new guinea pig better than I like Annabella! But I would like a new one."

"That reminds me, Dick. About the new guinea pig. That's the surprise. It's at home waiting for you and Annabella right now."

"Oh, Dad, really! A new sister and a new guinea pig, all at once. This is the best Christmas I ever had!"

ABOUT THE CHILD STUDY ASSOCIATION OF AMERICA

The Child Study Association of America is a national, nonprofit agency, founded in 1888 to further the education of adults in all that pertains to the well-being of children. Its program emphasizes improving the quality of family life in all kinds of communities, and training other members of the helping professions who work with parents and young people. The Association also publishes readable, informative books and pamphlets on various aspects of child care.

The Children's Book Committee of the Association carefully reviews all books published for children. It issues an annual list for the guidance of parents, and others with similar responsibilities, in selecting books for children. This story collection, and many others, welcomed by parents and children alike, has grown out of the committee's long years of experience in reviewing and evaluating books for children of all ages.

ABOUT THE ILLUSTRATOR

After a childhood on England's Yorkshire moors, Michael Hampshire studied art at the University of Leeds. He settled in the United States and later taught stage design at Marymount College in Tarrytown, New York. Mr. Hampshire is an experienced traveler, having journeyed through most of Europe as well as Ethiopia, the Sudan, Egypt, India, and Ceylon. The illustrator of many books for children, Mr. Hampshire is also an enthusiastic amateur archaeologist.

DATE DUE

2-B	JAN 6	FEB 5	3-D
5+	APR 17	APR 1	3-D
4-H	MAY 19	APR 28	3-D
2 M	OCT 28		3
Malcolm		SEP 25	6 P
2 5	FEB 15	OCT 14	6-P
1 P		SEP 27	3-B
3 L	DEC 2		
3-B	APR 12		
4 H	MAY 2		
6 P	DEC 9		
NOV 20	3 F		
MAY 2	3-S		
2-P	MAY 17		
	MAY 17		

1242

The Child Study Association of America
Pets and more pets